Five Years in Hell

Ariola Molla

Copyright © 2023 Ariola Molla

All rights reserved.

ISBN:979-8-218-34155-8

To Grace and Emma
May you have fancier secrets to tell your daughters.

FIVE YEARS IN HELL

CONTENTS

By way of a foreword xi
Part 1: What Is Happening, I Don't Understand 13
    Starting 14
    Collaboration 16
    Help! 17
    Practical Necessities 18
    Closure 19
    Where, Everywhere 20
    Dragged 22
    A Love Letter to my Kitchen 23
    Emma 24
    Step in, step out 25
    Functioning dysfunctions 26
    The Code 27
    Madness 28
    Instead of a Good Night 30
    Just Another Day 31
    Helplessness 32
    At the Edge with Emma 33
    The Nash Equilibrium 34
    Nothingness 35

Barefoot I Rise	36
The Lighthouse	37
Dices on a Tablecloth	38
Part 2: Darkness Falls Like the Night	40
Dented	41
The Martini Effect	42
The Party of Me	44
At the Sky Cafe	46
This Fabric	48
Eviction	49
Hey You	50
What to Do with the Past	51
Headache	52
Time	53
Of Living	54
Ashes	55
Where Do Memories Rest	56
I Might	57
Freedom	58
The Tale of the Waltzing Leaf Haunted by Darkness	59
Let me Sleep	60
This Caravan	61
Dear Mind	62

Listen God	64
Between a Sleepless Night and a Lipstick	66
Hey Stranger	67
Illusions	68
Walking with Jesus	69
Beethoven for a Day	70
This City!	71
Aliens & Places	72
If Only	73
Random Probability	74
Crowded	75
You Can Lie to Me	76
Deconstructed	77
Doors	78
Still	80
Is There an Angel Somewhere	81
The Paint on the Wall	82
The End of Thought	83
Stubborns	84
Listen God …Again	85
It Was Meant to Be Life	86
No Longer	87
As If	88
The Madhouse	89

Do I Look the Same to the Moon 90

Fractal 91

My Albanian Serenade Moment 92

Need an Apocalypse 94

Thank You to My Own 95

Lost All Appetite 96

Weight, Too Much Weight 97

Turn the Lights On 99

Part 3: He (Between the Abstract & the Singular) 101

The Music That Wasn't 102

Dreaming of a Beach 103

What Do You Mean My Love 104

Shapeless Desire 105

Not Lost 106

Good night 107

Who Cares 108

What Happened 109

First Coffee, Then Wine 111

Strolling the Seine 112

You Again! 114

If All of You Is All of Me 115

This Nonsense of Me, This Nonsense of You .. 116

Because You Don't End… 117

A Snowflake 118

Leave the Crowd of Me 119

When My Shadow Leaves 120

I Don't Mind it 121

Days Like This 122

Don't 123

Jamming with Strangers 125

How I Like It 128

Part 4: In Stubborn Search of a Smile 129

Inside Out 130

Another Drink 131

About a Wave and a Shore 133

Shut Up 134

Black in Pink 135

Grace's Secret 137

A Visit at the MET 138

Stories of the Living 139

Degrees of Separation 140

A Rainy Thursday in July Smelling like Cinnamon
 141

Structure of Me 142

Letter to Ferdinand Pessoa 143

A Christmas Wish 144

Listen Grace 145

On the Sideway 146

I start Friday with a Sunset 147

Guesses 148

Whose Company to Keep 149

Sunday Guesses 150

Silly Wishes 151

Hiking 152

At Some Point 153

Premium Fake 154

Wish I Could Invent a Language 155

A Heart with Boots 156

Just Don't Tell Me It's the Time of My Life 157

Smiles 159

Part 5: Hope or Something Like It 160

Mercy 161

Searching for a Poem Fallen from the Sun 162

Water-Shaped 163

Project X 164

Lunar Illumination 165

Guards to Executioners 166

Solve It! 167

A Birthday Card to Me 168

I Believe 170

On the Road Again 171

Writing & Erasing	173
In the Gangsters' Paradise	174
Inspire Me Please	175
No Right Card	176
You Always Can	178
Inevitably	179
I'm an Amateur	181
A Woman I Know	183
Why Do You Make Me Leave This Chair	185
Four Hours in Rome	186
I'll Fly	188
Effervescent	189
The October Diary	191
Pse Erdha	193
(The October has to speak in Albanian too)	193
Pretend Simple	195
ABOUT THE AUTHOR	196

FIVE YEARS IN HELL

By way of a foreword

This book was never intended to be written. Perhaps the only reason it is now published is to shape the legacy of hard years and bring into light and life an invisible world of emotions, an existence otherwise not existing. Paper, like Proust's memory, "would come like a rope let down from heaven to draw me up out of the abyss of not-being." Binding everything in a book felt like a debt I owed to myself, an existential need to look back and contemplate the past with the serenity of the present. Of course, it would be delightful if someone would find a moment to skim through its pages and I'd feel enormously privileged if I could bring someone with me through parts and pages of this journey. It will be a soulful conversation with everyone that has experienced and suffered long term emotional upheaval and injustice and a curiosity endeavor like visiting a new country for those lucky enough to have escaped chartering the edges of the psyche.

Part 1: What Is Happening, I Don't Understand

Starting

This is not an afterlife
I never passed for a dead
Breath was never just air
Life never truly left.

Wheels scream
A life ran over
Isn't it a wrong race
Can a mortal rule another's fate.

Wrong inception
Running too close to the burning bush
Are you that blind
Praying to the wrong gods.

There's something about existence
Within our walls govern kings we crown
There's no escape from the meaning
For the fool or the wise.

Nothing but pain
Left to breathe around the house
Pull the trigger
I can't stand it for too long
Too much heat
My chest suffocates
Schubert's madchen calling to chill.

I don't understand
I don't trust understanding
The wind whips in routines
As the night chews the day up
And I look for my phoenix

I've come this far
I must have one
Do I?

I'm an October run
Revolution or evolution touch
Elusive meanings
Take what u want
Returning favors we share this much.

Life still
I remember it different though
But I never passed for a dead
Do the dead know they're dead?

Collaboration

Madness or the illusion of it
What difference does it make
Meanings I can only play with
Am I the ridicule if I step in
Who cares
Joke's on all
And joke's on each
What am I saying
Joke's always been on me
I don't hear me laughing
How long can antagonism be avoided
With contradictions that don't yield.

Help!

I drove on top of every car
Jumped on the wings of a butterfly
On a motorbike held tight to a stranger
And afar from the shore gossiped with a wave.

Filtered the day in warm hues
Begged the wind to rip off an annoying kite
Negotiated with a crying baby
And spied on my heart for a smile.
….

Borrowed it all
Big and small
To deliver me to peace
The peace of an instant
A house in order for awhile
A war that ends
The joy of being alive.

Practical Necessities

My wallet got lost
Thought it was just me
Did I forget it somewhere
Or my hands yearned for a different touch
Questions of no importance now it seems.

I miss the bold reds
The soft feel of leather
As I miss myself - water and fire
The illusion of strength in the architecture of glass
That just like glass I shattered.

I regret the loss
Thought of no importance now it seems
Mostly a practicality
Yet practicalities I ignore
One can't see beyond own horizon
A practical thought after-all.

Someone called
Had found the wallet
It's on its way back
Only me now on the loose
And I wonder about me
As a matter of practical necessity.

Closure

The sent from above
I always thought of as mail
But words in the air I can no longer stand
I don't want to know
I don't want to hear.

Heavy doors
Falling loudly on yesterday
Is my only chance
For it I long
I beg
I pray.

Snow descended in silence
Does one really need noise to mark time
Can it freeze it
Or bleach it to forgetness
More white
I long for
I beg
I pray.

Where, Everywhere

Time demands acts
And I call on myself to sit next to me and do life
The chair waits in indifference
While low and high I search in despair.

I had become air
            Breathing everywhere
I had become pollen
            Falling everywhere
I had become water
            Running everywhere
I had become dust
            Scattered everywhere
I had become the universe
            Expanding everywhere.

I reach for the pieces
Jumping, crawling, running, staying
Laughing, crying, flirting, begging
Yet pieces through my fingers slip away.

How do I shape all in one
Or fold everything small enough to hug
Can the sky crumble into a single cloud
Or the pollen fall for a single tree
Or the water run after a single river
Can the universe let a single star fly free.

I look at the chair
It looks back at me
If only the dust could eat it away
Why would I want the self on its dead seat anyway.

Time's rushing me
And I search for myself again
If I can't have you here next to me
Can I escape
With you to be?

Dragged

Shortened under the weight of my head
Smaller next to its growing swell
In the ashes of its burning fires
Consumed by curses and desires.

My head on the ground
I can't stand the road dragging it along
I still race to beat the crowd
Still addicted to the horizon.

Bended a little
Anchored in the sun
Will I beat the day I wonder

It all depends on when I ask.

A Love Letter to my Kitchen

My kitchen gets me
And takes me
Then piece by piece puts me at ease

I bow to you fork
Hard are my nerves to untangle
Thank you knife
Cutting thoughts at every angle

Plates wear their patience thin
Scratching the air
Stop screaming for God's sake
Answers?
What's their realm?
Candy?
We've never served them

Harsh spot brave glasses between my pain and me
Sorry I threw you on the impossible ask
Of filtering reality

Unfiltered still remains
And no glasses unbroken left
Oh come on
Don't let me down
How can I carry
All the mess in my head.

Emma

She is the sun
The light that takes my hand each morning and walks me
to the day
The brightness I run to hiding from darkness
The heat that keeps my pieces melted in
The sun that sometimes goes down
Just to give me beautiful risings
Year around.

Step in, step out

I need a staircase
A ladder maybe
A bench might be just fine
Anything I can step in.

Maybe the moon's mysteries
Or my daughter's smile
Maybe the stories of the crazy ones
Or the poetry in wine.

Then along the cell walls
I might reach the window bars
Might even see light
Might even sense life from afar.

Like a hat
I'll throw the ceiling away
And my feet will murmur to the soul
If both can't leave, not both have to stay.

Steps of thought have short lives
Can't argue long, can't argue loud
Agree, disagree, always hurry
For God's sake, step in, step out!

Functioning dysfunctions

Many simulations get together in my polyverse
Working long hours
Lifting heavy weights
Inertia living without knowing why.

Sometimes they meet between shifts and breaks
Sipping espressos
Smoking occasionally
Filling up space with complaints.

The worker soothes in hand creams
The divorce lawyer and the client hold hands at the height of an argument
My beautiful dreamer went blind
Forgot all tales she knew forced out of light
There's the slave in chained pieces
And taking turns
The patient and the shrink.

The storm sent the roof away
A worn out blanket I pulled over my head
Pierced and patched
From its holes I savored the stars
And each night went to sleep
Dreaming of light.

The Code

The sky became my living room once
Its lightings were my reading lamps
And I tolerated thunder
Like background noise
Couldn't tell if the world under my feet
Was a paper tiger
Or a baby asleep.

Cracked the code I thought
Will send my head upstairs when the world throws evil a party
And maybe I'll add a new pair of glasses.

Why does it have to be this way
Why altruism on an evil bent
But let me have this moment for now
This moment I don't want to care.

Madness

> *"Madness is rare in the individual, but groups, parties, people and ages it is the rule"*, Nietzsche

Are you trying to tell me a story
Or write a new one
Of madness
Or entertainment maybe
I'm lost in this book and its pain constellation
Why have the saints forgotten this place.

I see
I hear
I ache
I hate it all
I fear holding on to the moment for long
Its darkness scares me
I fear asking
Yet silence I can no longer afford
Nor denial
That'd be sanity abandoning me
Or did it already happen
Am I myself or the runaway shadow
Life allows no vacuum, doesn't it
In empty spaces
I see madness rushing in.

I fell on a page
Trying to fly away
Ironic isn't it
Just a coincidence perhaps
Madness is rare in the individual
It rules groups it read
I hugged myself
And took her away

Not mad I laughed
Not us
Not today.

Instead of a Good Night

All my life have hated roller coasters
Now I can't get off one
Maybe that's why I never tried
Who needs the toy when you're stuck on a real one.

No landings in sight
How did I end up here
With the ticket I didn't buy.

Hey
Thanks for the ride
I'm still dizzy
Yet in each mile
I met myself as I never had
I fascinate me with my infinity
Now I want off
Why still on the edge
Where is it taking me next.

Just Another Day

> *"Leave me but a little to myself"*
> *Othello*

Illusions of meaning
    The meaning of noise
        The noise of tears
            The tears of falling
                Falling behind
                    Behind and low
                    Where wires bend

                    Tell me God
                    Does it ever end.

Helplessness

To think or not
I am
So I think
Yet I can't keep the walk
So I fall
Still can't help thinking
Up on my feet still can't walk
So I fall
Still can't help thinking
The helplessness of it all.

At the Edge with Emma

Do I know you now
I don't think I do
Where was I if I never left
Did I forget you next to me
Too busy with tomorrows
In this walk I brought you in.

Life next to mine
Shattering my illusions
Realities too
Can I be your home
Can you be my travel
I don't know where to meet
What balance to hold on to
Sitting now at the edge with you.

Shall I say I'm sorry
If better's no choice
Would you understand
My heart's doing the speaking
There's always a choice you insist
Yes
And
It always lives inside the borders of our existence.

The Nash Equilibrium

> *The Nash equilibrium supposes full knowledge*
> *of all potential moves to reach optimal*
> *decisions.*

I'll go for a book of paradoxes when the park is far
Contradictions only to understand
Not solve
Easier than my life's hand
Asking to solve
What I can't understand.

Nonsense words that hold no reason
In brutal architecture
Heart and mind sores
Yet naive is the listener.

In vain I search for the Nash equilibrium
In yet another paradox
of choices in the vacuum
I search I don't know what
I surrender
And go back
To the book of paradoxes that make sense
The reading that I can understand.

Nothingness

Why so many words
To tell me nothing
Shouldn't nothing be silence
Things I see
More I hear
I see me too
Melted in your nothingness
What verse do I live in.

Chatted with a dead friend in my sleep
Hadn't heard how are you in so long
Palpable even the thought.

I walk around the city
Are you still standing asks the day
Loud as a clash
And you-
It's nothing
Is all you still say.

Barefoot I Rise

A storm wiped me off
Questions still open-ended
Endings still opened
Like people still talk hell
Since creation.

How do I count black on white on God's design
The reading of a day
Or that of a lifetime.

Slammed on the shore
The air I breathe runs out hot
Wait, don't leave
What did you see inside tell me.

Half alive
Heavy with the storm
Slowly I rise up
And barefoot leave its shore.

The Lighthouse

I didn't see myself coming at you
Busy as I was
Reading dreams
And escaping the day
As I usually do.

The daylight reveals surroundings
Certainties follow each instant
I don't understand this strange thrill
Of the lighthouse in the distance.

I'm somewhere
Amidst people and thought
Is there something happening
Should I pretend as if nothing at all.

This life bothers me
I search for a new dimension
A new simulation
But why should I waste my days on a search.

I didn't know I was lost
When I felt your light pulsating in my blood
Like a fate mark on my way
Telling of the unfortunate distance that still waits.

Dices on a Tablecloth

This place is about to close
Guests have left
Forgetting stories behind
Or taking with them the forgetting
A guitar serenades a few tables down
While the white tablecloth in front of me begs for its own story.

Why am I laughing
I can write on tablecloth
Shaping this moment into its own monument
The thought can go to sleep after I stamp in words
It's my new niche
Another way of marking time
Like another lovelock on the bridge.

I can only take you a few lines a day
If I wish to wake up on this side of life
Quick bartender please
First need to finish my drink
Then use an air affair
With the past heavy on my throat
And hot on my tongue the day.

Face to face
I know mine
Can I hear your name
Say it out loud
Christ, this is a laugh house
Wish I knew sooner
Now I don't see light
Just the lightness of paper flying.

Did I stretch the moment for too long
Damn, my sin
How do I get thoughts now to set me free
I seek distance
And I'm no God to rule on uncertainties.

… An end
That eludes with a different face each day
Like a dice roll hit
Isn't it absurd
To have dice rule a life that doesn't come in repeat.

Part 2: Darkness Falls Like the Night

Dented

On an anger diet for too long
Waterfalls inside my chest running heavy and wild
Can't help punching the walls of time
Fists of rage denting hours.

Same dish
Like clock hands comes around
Monotonous, bland
How to serve indifference back.

The belt of words moves in circles
A carousel of smirks flying high and low
Nothing but hurt
Nothing but an ugly show.

My head's dizzy
My anger sober
Is it the drink or your reflection on it
I beg me to slow down
Hide the mind from the sick.

Reality –
World in front of us
World inside us
All dimensions suffocate
How do I knock down your world
Wiping its dust off my heels
And tap dancing the ruins away.

The Martini Effect

I love thinking of an espresso martini
And all the things it will do to me
The little soul dance
The pleasure of chats afterwards
The sparkles rushing in
A flash of truth
A flash of dream
A flash of thrill
My beautiful forever heartache
I'll be your moon orbiting you forever.

Happy I drown
Poisoned in its elixir-
Of thought or liquid alike
My obituary would casually get rid of me
Cause of death - the Martini effect
My laugh will stir up the water
Raptures of the deep for a float
Since when
From the lands of Bacchus I come
Pleasure courts wine stolen from Gods.

My curses heavy around my neck
With the serenity of the surface I go
With all the longing for the depth
Lucky I feel contemplating my quest
I tolerate death
Death doesn't tolerate me yet.

Riding waves of doubt
Thunder shatters my feet
Too high this wall of bitterness
The otherside always a miss

Stuck underwater
Will I know to walk the shore again.

I don't die
I don't live
The lesser evil it's hard to guess
This empty paper only invites like a mirror
Not an oracle to tell.

The Party of Me

All wrong
I walk through dark days
In bright hours I go to sleep
How do I align with light
When the walls around hide the switch.

No answer
No one listens
Or waits for a turn to speak
Only voices
Too many voices
Slapping my solitude in whips.

The heart runs for a nook to cry
The hands tremble on a gossip chord
The eyes dream what they can't see
And the chest can barely hold
Like spies
The lungs slow down to listen
Ever more slow
As they've forgotten to breathe.

The carnival stepped over wires
And the lights died
Is life next
Oh come on
Bring the disco lights
Let's dance
Don't stop
Maybe a bath later on.

I sway to the serenade
Ridiculing limits

No sounds beat my eardrums
And I still dance
Who cares when the heart's listening.

Desperate to reinvent
Yet the journey reinvention defies
The same map haunts me down like a lunatic
Like a lunatic I dance around fire.

The party's still on
Unfathomably so
I got nothing to do with it
Just the power of life
Still burning fire.

At the Sky Cafe

I.
I boarded a plane
Craving a flight in ages
Emptied heart and mind at the gate
And left goodbyes on a doormat of pains.

My father, my grandma waived from the sky cafe
By a sun-bite table
Full of lucid dreams
If only I could stay here forever.

The present
Off-present life can afford
The past or the dreams
I need this absurdity
Please don't land in.

Time stands still in the air
No disturbances
How much sun in your drink
Feel free to try
Maybe some are meant to walk and some to fly.

Pull a chair for God if he passes by
I need a celestial code reset
It's not the sunset burning in the sky
Neither my wine spilling red
Just my heart bleeding empty
Don't you see
The gravity that was lost
Flew me up here.

II.
They put the moon on my eyes

Stars in my glass
Sunbeams we smoked
Like breakfast before a long way back.

I refuse
Life exists in the move
I can't break the wheelchair
It is breaking me
No father
I'm not leaving
Mortals can be our game for once
Maybe finally we'll catch a laugh.

III.
Fragile
Oh so fragile
My daughters walk through the fog
Confused like falling meteors
Can I be an audience I wonder
Afterall, isn't it trivia
Now or later
We all die.

You can't contemplate future
From the shallows of the present
Father said
Like light
Souls rise each day
Let the night teach you of the dark
And hold the hand of God walking until dusk.

Did my father win this round?
My daughter texts a poem
And unwilling or annoyed I can't tell
I fly down.

This Fabric

This fabric
So fragile
Woven in patches and thin pieces
So magical
It still holds me
A fireball of volcanoes and earthquakes
Like the Aladdin's carpet
High above emotions
Building skyscrapers on troubled waters.

Tells me stories at its leisure
Even showed me a man the other day
Ripping my stomach apart
I don't understand its muses
I never can
I just dust off the story
And fly to finish the man.

Eviction

This moment is mine
And I am this moment
And the one before it
The one after it too
Be careful where you step
There're my broken pieces all around
And my thoughts next to my glasses.

This moment is my home
The order unfolds its tenets on descend
Waiving its flag on the roof
Trespassing forbidden
This moment is my home
The space's taken
It's time for you to leave!

Hey You

Hey you
Don't hurt too much
Flexing hard to understand
There's not a lot
Just men without bibles playing gods
Don't whip yourself down on their feet
Stop cursing yourself
Theirs is the sin
Lift you up
Gently
Let the demons asleep
In the night hours take you to the park
With the falling leaves and the changing seasons
You'll be reminded of the only God.

Hey you
Love yourself
Melt it all in Christmas drinks
You can do it
Yours is a magic gift.

What to Do with the Past

A heartache slows me down
And I need to sit
Listen to it for awhile
Afterall, in the darkness of the night
I can only see clear inside
I can only hear my own tide.

Shuffling photos in a parking lot
What past to keep
Yes, no, maybe
I'm not a hoarder
Only tired under stacks of ugly pasts
Help me with a lighter
Here's paper for a bonfire.

I used to be good with numbers
Now walking vectors backwards
Everything weights like a minus
Can beauty still fit in my lines.

I still wait for late mail
Time's a post office that never rests
Not too much longer
It's getting late in the parking lot
And the day's calling my name
I need to ride on.

Headache

How much circus can one really watch
It soon becomes a bore talent for the eye
Ding-dong
Noise
Too much noise
Heard and seen it all before
Why does it never get tolerably old
This fabric of stories
Can I exchange it for freedom
I'm the Merchant of the Self
Memories I don't need
Let me weave them in a rag
And walk over it
With no return.

Time

What's the calendar for the day
Will let this horse choose the ride
Can't do much on my own
Wounded
Like a blanket
On his back
Thrown.

My father used to serenade about white horses
Reminded him of love
Transcendence to light
Blinded by pain
I can't feel the color of the time horse
Just praying
It won't miss the sunrise.

Of Living

Thinking of living
Is like inviting an earthquake
Deafened by the blast
Watching your heart
Cracking long and deep
Like a mountain
Falling apart
Falling in
Rocks shattering
The pain grid all lit
Sitting heavy on your scream
Why thinking
Why living
Which of the two is to blame
Has the discussion indeed any merit.

Ashes

How does misery look
So that I can change street
Next time I spot it
Is it like the ashes of a house
- The disappearance of life certainties
Or like the ashes of a cigarette
- The slow death of an illusion you carelessly smoked in
Perhaps the ashes of fire you set yourself
Are the ultimate misery
Sensibilities lost
There's no poetry in ugly talks
Just bitterness swallowing my mouth
Can it all fit back in the empty Marlboro
Like this hill of ashes
That begs for more.

Where Do Memories Rest

I suspect all memories
Sleep in blood
And blood sleeps
When memories run
Some pact of power sharing
Speech rights for the past and the present
Where the ordinary is forgotten
Only storms wave high and low
Sometimes too harsh
Too wild
Breaking out
Sometimes the reds can be sunsets
Sometimes just blood spilled out.

I Might

I might lose my mind to the wind
Or my breathe to the bars on my chest
Or fall in its chasms
In an instant I might go with no notices passed
In awe I look at the mirror
And no fear I see
Absurd the thought of it.

I stand at peace
In ease I walk beyond
My God
Are you proud of me.

An ordinary moment
Forgotten by the next one
No firsts down this line
Life's a gamble anyway
The joke of fates' playing
My daughters perhaps will miss me
Crying with the willow tree on my stone
They won't hear my tears from its other side
How I wish I could hold them longer!

Freedom

It's dark under the sun
Perhaps a celestial error
An oxymoron fit for a story
Perhaps a new toy on the God's shelf-
The sun wears a black mask.

Is it a laugh or a thought that I'm still hearing
Thanks for the company
None is needed
A freedom run is all I'm seeking
That 100th line or so in the Webster
Or in some law verse
Though too many words I don't need like trees hiding the sun
I dream the clarity of the desert
Easier
To be alone
Easier
To be together.

The Tale of the Waltzing Leaf Haunted by Darkness

Homeless
Under a roof
Mad
Still not happy
By the ocean
Thoughts are all I can wash
A looser
Sporting Aventus Creed
A mother
With a daughter cooking meals.

I write to understand
Yet I write in the dark
The habit of curving letters
The only guide on my hand
What am I writing
Do I even understand.

Maybe I'm a falling leaf
Waltzing under the sky
Worrying over lipstick and heels
Flying off casually with the wind.

Let me Sleep

Trying to lose grip of the evening
And fall asleep
I can't
Who thought losing would be so hard
Or falling would need conscience acts
And I don't mean semantics.

Have I not yet earned the forgetting
Let me in
I don't ask for much
No feasts of bounty
Or dreams
No fortune teller chats.

Throw me like a beggar
I don't care
In dark nooks
Over cold steps
Or let me be your joker
Just let me fall asleep
Just take me somewhere away from me.

This Caravan

A caravan walks around with me
In circles
The exit's lost.

They speak
They show up
Can you stop for a moment
Can I catch a breath
They disappear with smirks
Now here
Where next.

Mirrors crumble on me
Endless glass on broken skin
What passion is draining off-
The suffering or the dreaming?

Dear Mind

Don't make of me a towel on the sand
I came with one
If there's a different beach you want
We can dream it together
Walk it perhaps
I just beg you
Don't let go of my hand.

Don't be the forever convenience store
Chasing around attention demand
And after hours open floors
Not your calling
Don't break the lamp
And don't let go of my hand.

I'm lonely, not alone
Pain's not bored of me yet
Would you remain for the ride
We leave together as we came in
Let's wheel in reverse these lines.

If there's no will left
Muscle it
If there's no muscle
Dream it
You're my favorite homeland
I beg you
Don't let go of my hand.

I might not know why I ask you this
The future I remember is always dark
The forever of the moment too
If you'd give up I'd understand

But please, I beg you
Don't let go of my hand.

Listen God

I came all the way up here
To reach you
Closer
Louder
Freer.

Save me
I've been carrying this cross for too long
Not that I know what else to do with it
And these crowds even longer
Not that I see other options.

And if you can't
Then watch over me
As I silent my walls
While I shatter inside
As I keep the lights on
While darkness devours like the night mountains.

And if you can't
Then revenge me
They turned this city into my slaughterhouse
Watching me bleed on psycho hooks and piano wires
I ride with Valkyries to deafen the pain
They're the Medusa to go under.

Listen God
Give me all three
Can't be less angle for life to have a shape
Level their hills like the horizon line
With nothing left behind.

Listen God
Life I never lived
Only life I suffered
Some days worse than others
Life, freedom, redemption
For both of us to make sense
Life, freedom, redemption
NOW.

Between a Sleepless Night and a Lipstick

I can't sleep
Can't tell if my head or chest burns hotter
Can't own the night
The life that left
Forgot the pain behind
I'm still here
Walking the halls of time and existence
Counting miles
While the lipstick in the hiking bag
Reads 'Live a Little'.

Hanging on the skyline
Too tired of the walk
I miss the echo of laughter off wine crystal
Not airing too much monologue.

I dream of taking down walls
Behind them reaching for life
Touch love perhaps
Dinner before or after
Still lipstick for each after
Where is the hiking bag.

Hey Stranger

How shall I fight this
Don't ask what
Stop pretending behind the marble over your bones
Not a shape of life dissolving in the air
Useless is the light.

Tell me
How do I get my hands
On the sword that knows no rest inside my mind
To end the street
Before it ends me still alive.

I won't conquer
I know
And yet
Desire that wears no act
Burns down its own castle
And I don't want that.

Get something inside my head
As this other death does
If there's no sword to give me
Keep me guessing
You and me on both sides of this marble
As darkness passes by.

Illusions

Where is the spring
Left it here yesterday
Did the rain burn it
Can't figure it through the smoke
I hope not
It's my palace
Not much else I can walk back to
All burnt down long ago
Only the dead still lounge around
I need the spring couch!

At the edge of the moment
At the mercy of anxieties
Not even the thought opens to the sky
I sway on rain ropes
Waiting for the day in some shape and form to smile.

Then at least
I can lay my eyes on the illusion that's my life
Like this deer running high on quiet fields
Was it a dream
Or did it just move like one
Now there
Next here.

Walking with Jesus

I met you in secret
Over broken thought and red egg shells
That my grandma forgot behind
I let you in
And you made me power
The anchor in fleeting joys and emptying sadness
The quiet weight of air
And relentless bird singing.

Christ is risen I hear
If I reach for your hand
Will you raise me too
What is a Savior for
If hell runs my house
Did you leave to save yourself
At least
I can understand that.

Shall I let you go
Leave the church for a temple
Sisyphus never left after all
I don't even know how to read this thought I was sent
Assertion of power or
The ultimate resignation itself.

Beethoven for a Day

A silent present hanging still
While I'm crocheting thoughts
Can still kill
The certainties of stagnation invite unknowns
Afterall, what difference does the cause make
If breathing still fails on the cradle of a thought I can't seem to finish
Better if I leave this bed.

Wish I could blame time forgetting to walk
Or the Beethoven that I'm stuck in singing-
An unimportant detail of the day you'd think
Like some candle flickering
Symphonies in D
The best written perhaps Lamentations
Sonatas in C
Moonlight
Pathetique yes
It's again me.

Wish I could blame me
Too drunk to go out on the street
Or lost deep in dreams
Yet the hall of broken mirrors
Throws another riddle
Why not?
Versailles is still open for business.

Beethoven, let me be you for a day
How to walk outside if not deaf
I need a masterpiece
Through all shapes and no paths
Need to compose a rhythm for my heart.

This City!

"Knowing me, knowing you, it's the best I can do."
ABBA

Headaches have me for breakfast
Usually they take the seat of dreams
Before espresso rendezvous
Or mail delivery
The city grinds leftovers in its mills
Persistently
Devoid of reason I can see
I don't get it
Force of habit perhaps
Like a heart that still beats
After life has left
Can I put an order
Have these mills blast into dust
Blinding the talks
Or is the city blind after all
If it doesn't see the madness of its walks.

Aliens & Places

I don't recall temptation
Moving down my street
Can't care less about transcendent maps of thought
Perhaps transcendence wants to know me.

Seeing there
Resting here
I walk on water
Yet I fear
Another step
Another block
Will it be a ride or a fall.

I can't read uncertainties
I hurt
Yet condolences are impossible
Except for tears chasing the walk
I hear them knocking
Wish it's just alcohol eroding walls.

Better not leave this beach
Or this argument with my daughter
Doubts pave the water
A few certainties as well
Like the history's suggestion that
Places and aliens can't stand each-other
Except in regret.

(Mexico 2021)

If Only

I can excuse its flames
If I can rest on this moment a bit longer
I fear more the next one rolling in
One can only crash when they're falling.

I don't want to leave this tree
Or the sunlight I'm drinking to ease the noise behind my back
If only I can lean on it a bit longer
Eating time and sky chunks
Like cotton candy fluff.

Random Probability

> *Because I'm tired of hearing 'what doesn't kill you makes you stronger.'*

Missing hits are just pain that leaves
Or something like this they say
The daily poison story I suppose
And I wonder
If simple muscle is the soul.

Nonsense wouldn't work
Not for long anyways
Neither can pain be the seduction or the whip
For a heart that pain bleeds.

These things we tell ourselves when we mourn
Why we love the comfort that foregoes the loss
This selective reality
Doesn't it make for a weak soul.

A hit that misses
A hit that kills
Is it really soul fitting
Or a matter of random probability.

Crowded

Can't turn down the volume of my head
Street music does nothing either
So loud its echo
There're the pills
And I grab the wine
Like it better how it moves on me
Its taste and stories on my lips.

Been looking at pain for so long
Pain is lonely
But loneliness is crowded
A new world born inside my head
I reach for the paper
I don't know why
Does it make me forget or feel alive
On its fields too many words now
I allude myself that weight is gone
The echo's left.

You Can Lie to Me

Time has me in speed dial
Shooting dreams at dawn like daily logs
It broke the ally streak
Gossip's just third-party talk
Why know of the hit you can't stop.

Power asymmetries
Inspire thoughts of getting even
Neither history suggests better
Out in the street
I have no admiration for the bigger
I measure power by its soul
And see none in a hit
I take shelter where I find it
Can't love what pains me
Reciprocal is my symmetry.

So time
Be smooth
I don't need oracles of hit
A few mutual exchanges I beg for
Accept my deal
A script of mine
For each one I receive
Deliver my dreams
In all verses I don't see
Or at least give me the satisfaction
Of dreaming their delivery
Yeah, you can lie to me.

Deconstructed

Past liver
These bottles can now hold candles
Tall
Like pine trees in a graveyard
What's next
What sacrifices to offer for time blessings
Where do I rest
Swinging on cigarette smoke
Why there's so much talk
So many faces
Inside my mind
I need a prayer
Better a lullaby
Enough reading
Who needs more reading
Truth's the lip of the mouth that rolls it
I don't even run my day
It will be run over anyway.

Doors

I found the doors
That throw off chambers the thought
In truth
The doors found me
Beaten
Pushed around
Baptized in unbecoming.

Deafening slams
Where am I off to
Dead in cold
Born in heat
Dead in flames
Scattered in fog.

Back by the window now
Did time pass
What time is
Do the feet
Or the soul measure it
Dripping off the road
Feet never left the ground
The joke of an alibi!

Doors
Not a string of beads monotony
Chaos threw too many miles on me
Loose on the floor now
Are clothes and beads.

Busy with passersby
And lazy espresso sips
Leaning on the frame -

Of a reference or the window still
Thunders I hear in my chest
And wind gulping in
A door must be opened somewhere.

Still

Life moved out one day
Or the street moved in
Seasons have changed
Yet sameness here holds still
Fragile
Like fine china along the sideway
Where strollers pick the hit
From the other side of happiness.

I've lost sight of it
Where can it be now
What love
What party
What dress & heels
What vanity carousel it's riding in?

Worlds collide
Illusions crash
Will it walk back
Will I know it still
And I count my steps on the ground
Like a certainty I don't want to miss.

Is There an Angel Somewhere

Trying to escape worlds-
That inside
That outside too
Each throwing me helpless toward the other
On an horizontal track of pain
That like horizontal women
Follows lights
Darkness too
Stretching to the highest bid of time
Indulging in pretense
While sheers on the floor
Loop around a man's neck.

Can't show much of it around either
The world needs a different touch
A different cloth
No- nonsense frames on the wall.

Freedom lost to pain
My God, what I've seen
There must be an angel somewhere
To look over me.

The Paint on the Wall

If you're my pain
You can't be the healing
The bullet can't heal its wound
Can only fool in pretend
Like the illusionist with dazzling ribbons
Or the word of the court
Masquerading in season
The utilitarian perhaps
With buckets of paint pollocking empty canvas.

Pain
Not paint
Why do I deceive myself
Isn't there enough
Have I forgotten any better
It's a blood tax
Not an art one.

Open wallets again
More champagne now
Under Moulin breeze one more toast
Before the curtain goes down.

I wish time could delete this act
I know it won't
Time's a dimension, not a fleeting act
The nakedness has nowhere to go
Or beautify itself
God allows no changes on its walls
Just spare me a bottle
I need to forget.

The End of Thought

Forests for empires
Rooftops for the stars
Searching God becoming God
It never ends
Our lives -
A relentless thought march.

Except in my world
Where thought ended
Not in pain or a car crash
No rat run inside a ball
It walked to its end
And left nothing behind
Like paper burns into ash
Or day dies into night.

I walked back
Perhaps not what the proverb said or meant
But still couldn't stop its ringing
It's madness to join dead ends.

How long can one carry on fiction living
I ask leaning on the bookshelf
Waiting for time to reveal answers
When time doesn't even reveal itself.

Stubborns

Lost in thought
For how long I don't remember
Not lost
Just on a different map
Wandering
Either feet or thought
Running this watch.

Stubborns...
Like everything else
The pain and the spring bloom
Nothing leaves
Nothing skips an entrance
Do we end when the crowd gets too big.

I'm no exception
Stubborn like all that is
This playground you enter once
Want to waste my time on favorite ice cream.

Am I free
I need to be free.
Good morning to everything!

Listen God ... Again

I'm lost on these hills
And their wilderness
Why can't I be my own compass
I count a few degrees
And a Fulbright
That's the end of the pride.

A dropout line in my resume too
The push adds to the gravity of the fall
And it's okay
I vaguely remember
Any past behind the present
Afterall.

Wish I could take a selfie
Call it a memory
So that the present could be shelved like yesterday
Hate this fervor of throwing life away
But what else is left to do
Smoke's all that covers my trail.

Listen God
Hundreds of pages soak in sadness out of my tired lungs
Let me write of happiness
For once.

It Was Meant to Be Life

Meant to be mine
Meant to be life
As time one counts usually is
You made it a search for one
Or a march to death
Same things I feel.

Timeless
While mine runs out
On absurd maps
While I still carry heart and mind
Crusades fought in my soul
While I never gave a lien on mine.

Yeah you got laughs
And serious prescriptions
Bipolar screamed a side of my wall
Isn't it so flattering
After all this time
I'm still able to escape the fatal pole.

Dragged myself all this way for a human hand
The abyss it's too much to understand
Yet all I could reach
All that could reach me
Were deceitful herds.

I cried of course
Easy to play with others' pains
Cynical celebrations ring loud on the street
While I sit shuffling a small catalogue of feelings.

(Miami 2022)

No Longer

No longer I understand the warm breeze
Or the pale moonlight on the shore
The soft crushing of waves
The tenderness of it all.

This starry night
It alone 's holding my head up
Have I ever seen it before
For too long its beauty was lost.

Magician the night lighting up my soul
Give me more
Send the sleep away
There's no rush
The chameleon of the day can wait.

Clocks can run just the same
Arithmetic with no head
Confused folks would be flipping agendas in the night
And I'd laugh-
I changed the world tonight.

Too beautiful a thought
Too much nobility
All too distant
It's why I give it no care
My peace is the kingdom I'm after
And if a little night is all I got
Its hours will be the stones on the walls tonight.

(Mexico 2022)

As If

Ended the last chapter
One never knows where life pages rest
But I feel its story ended
Or I lost interest
No freelance yet
As if still asking something from me
In meetings that never end
Full of nervous laughs and arrow fights
Too zealous of a hurt.

Around the corner
The concert escapes me too
Unless it's tears
I'm a foreigner now
I can't see through.

Mark me absent
'Permit to leave' scribble on my seat
The sound of my steps walking away hears like a dream
Life still denies
As if still asking something from me.

The Madhouse

It wouldn't be a madhouse
If everyone waited to be seated
Or there were private doors

Not a madhouse
If not for the aimless wandering around
With no wind to hide
And no broken mirrors to encrypt reflections

It's truth what I'm seeing
Not a madhouse
If not this city.

Do I Look the Same to the Moon

Have I said this all before
So what
The finite alphabet limits its constellations
Same pains limit the thought
First coffee then wine
Straight to wine this time
Not awake
Not asleep
The truth won't knock too loud
Like a waning moon
Most lost in the dark.

What is the weight on my chest
Like a mountain it can't walk
Is it a tear stuck inside perhaps
Or a river rushing down my veins
With its exit lost.

A life of grace was my dream
Now only my daughter carries the name
Yeah, thanks God for the life chance
I'll toast with time at the end.

Neither life nor grace in front of me
Just the moon jumping on clouds
And I can't help thinking
Do I look the same to her
After all these years and rounds?

Fractal

Grace do not interrupt
Just let me finish
I need this flight
You know me
I can't escape the alchemy of shadows mapping the sky.

A wire fence is all I see in front of me
Its thorns in perfect repetition are the only certainty
Life's in the distance
Veiled in ash
The kind of heavy one that travels through time
Still unsettled
Left Santorini behind
And still no Atlantis.

Wish I could take this ride
Wish I could distance the distance of life
The wire's the last memory
That the tears on windows carry in their fall
Or is its memory rolling them down afterall
I don't understand what the wind's saying
My heartbeats are too loud
Angry with the metal taste of my blood.

The world becomes small
Fractal at each cut
Storms following like Russian dolls
Still think I can take this ride
Resting my hope on my father's name
St. Theodore's the day
Faith has got to be my breastplate
I take the ride
Anyway.

My Albanian Serenade Moment

Vodha dikur nje kitarre
Mu kujtua sot s'di si
Neper endrra humbur
Shume urova te me kendonte lumturi.

Pas lirise renda
Humba veten pas cdo pragu
E lashe mendjen nder fjalore
U dogja nder deshire
Mes gishtash rodhen vec lot.

Nder lote harrova jeten
Linda a vdiqa me dhimbjen nuk di
As diference nuk kuptoj
Ditet rane mbi tela, u thermuan ne hi.

Kenge te paftuara
Dialogje nate nuk pushojne ne dhomen time
Ku jam une?
E varfra kenga ime e lirise
Qe qiejt nuk i preku kurre.

Nder tehe ankthesh mu pre fryma
Ta humbja ne puthje enderroja dikur
Krevatin e dua nen diell
Me nje rreze te genjej jeten sikur.

Kam frike te qesh
Nuk do di te pushoj
Te jem cmendur valle
Ne me kane ngelur lot
Orteku i kujtimeve do me hedhe ne cmendine
Kam kaq frike te qaj.

Ne ajer ngrita strehen time
Vallezova me stuhi dhe ere
Ne dyer spitalesh u rrezova
Pyes veten, s'kuptoj me jete.

As kuptoj
As ndjej
Koha ime shkruar ne variacione dhimbjesh
Ne s'mund rrishtaz ta filloj dot kete jete
A mund te harroj
A mund te jetoj
Sikur s'kam jetuar asnjehere.

Need an Apocalypse

Everything so empty
Full of dust at once
Like this noise
And this day
Numbed I walk
Can't find even a shirt to turn a nerve on
What's the point of all these stores.

The white's my only serenity shield
Libation alterations –
Yes, there is that
Hennythings
What else
Damn, I need an apocalypse.

Got no patience for a book
Prefer my thoughts to others'
I surrender mine to the water
Its chill
Still cuts through my clouds
Its velvet
The intimacy of sheets passes on me
And I feel alive
It's more life than the city allows.

Thank You to My Own

Reading is of no use to me now
The letters caravan holds no treasures of peace
Through dust it drags me to the end
Lends me this white page
Where my own verses
Still awake
Wait under the book cover
To hold me
Foregone the boredom of explaining
As they see me through
In their voice
I found peace
I make no sense of this cursed life
At least they make sense of me.

Lost All Appetite

Texts didn't stop
As you said it would
Do you want my glasses to read
'Gone are chances to life
If music is left behind'
I don't know about truth
The feeling for it long vanished
And it kills me.

The smell of fried oil nearby soaks the air
Between the said and the unsaid
Lost all appetite
While my thoughts run the Adriatic like wave ropes.

Still anchored by the water
I walk to my luggage
Aren't thoughts supposed to arrive before the steps
I don't want to leave
I can't move
As the anchor weighs heavy on my chest.

(Durres 2023)

Weight, Too Much Weight

All broken
And I break again
All I hear is the sound of my breaking
While the world stands still
Is there even a world left for me to exist.

I still stand
On my mountain of the broken
A madness tyranny down at my feet
Not just madness, more
Not just tyranny, more
In separation they can't exist.

Let there be silence if not peace
Let it all die
The emotional melt of my family
And the annoyances of the street
Neither soul nor head can forever beat short circuits.

Distractions to happiness
Suggested my therapist
A nod for the poetical attraction
Another for the wisdom series
But why a default of misery.

Never understood if pain is thirsty
Or the hope prefers drinking
I look for something to fool me into deceptions of ease
Doesn't matter what
I crave something red
Something strong.

What is to 'hold the world'
A lifestyle of no life
Or a daily workout routine
Meanings morph into singularities
Weight, too much weight, is all I feel.

Turn the Lights On

Where am I
I remember sirens and straps cutting the night
Infinity mirrors and mosaics twisting behind my eyes
What did the dream say
All so real
Help me out
I don't remember much
What was in the pill.

My blood's running weak
My feet still pretend on an elliptical of water and decaffeine
Pump it all up
I don't care heart or mind
I forget the errand
Praying that some of me will survive.

Depression
Paranoia
Enough
Two points draw a line
A line I don't cross
Forget insistence
I'm not much into coloring
Just fluent in the geometry of existence.

Walls of cedar and honey...well
That I never understood
Not autumn's flavors on a roll
Do they defend me
Or deny me the world.

Performers, get off the ladder
Quite a piece
I don't run after my thoughts
And send silence on a spree
Right now
Right here
It only takes a pen to feel free.

If only I had a glass of wine
Of fresh air the second best
Perhaps demons would be dancing, perhaps
Turn on the lights now
This is the end.

Part 3: He (Between the Abstract & the Singular)

The Music That Wasn't

Chasing down thoughts climbing off the walls
And others out of the gate
Silly songs
Leave me alone
My own mazes at least takes me somewhere
At the end of a thought
At the end of the day.

Don't sling me to the whirlwinds of the Bermuda
Triangle
Where Jamaica used to be in another life
Until I accidentally moved it
In the maps somewhere around my heart and mind.

Capriccios of fate or game
Reckless either way
Molded of life
Yet life they can't give back
Silly little songs
Joker's no-show act?

Still bleeding
Still healing
I can crack a branch
I can break a triangle.

Careless songs
I can try my hand at a deal
Perhaps a part of me will be left in your rhythm
So will your scar on my skin
I want to laugh at it all
Can you also throw a laugh in?
(Miami 2021)

Dreaming of a Beach

Still dark outside when I woke up
Opened the windows
Trying to catch the beauty of wandering dreams
No use ignoring knockings on the glass
Or the shattering waterfalls in me
Can I tie the cascade in a vase
And roll out their ropes
To catch pelicans flying over waters
Until I reach a beach
And lay down on a shore
Will you come with me
Will you be my shore.

What Do You Mean My Love

You're the word of love
That heavens wrote to me
Or perhaps a half
Fallen off the sky
Searching for the other
Reading lips after lips.

I chased you like a butterfly
Swallowed the fluttering
Sometimes I forget I'm alive
I need a reminder
I need the wings inside.

My sweet word of love
Or half word
Speak to me
What's a word that says nothing
Is it even a word if I don't hear it.

I can only become in you
You can only become in me
Where you start
Where I end
I don't know
We're just heaven talking to itself.

Shapeless Desire

There's this other presence in my room
The shape of my desire
A desire that lost shape
Like the air to fill all around.

It laughs with me
We can only collide in this small room of mine
I suffocate under its weight
And grab its mouth to breathe me back to life.

My head's falling of the pillow
Can you move just a bit?
Where did u go, come back
I didn't ask for you to leave!

Like legends
We don't get smaller either
The world needs to become the room
What other options for such existence.

Do you want to crush
I want to know transcendence
Maybe then my pieces would fall together
And I can leave this world in the warmth of an embrace.

Not Lost

I'm lost in you
Don't know how
And I speak God
The universe is my playground
I lose voice partying with clouds.

Walking along these walls you built
Of chalk and songs
I stop by their paintings
Color hits me with no light
Impressionism that doesn't impress
All in the hiding.

I lean on the walls
They fall behind me
Can one get lost
By emptiness surrounded
The business of leisure
Not always the best
So sad to breathe life just to tell.

Good night

Almost crashed my car
Steering thoughts along foggy tracks
Good night
Maybe sheets will wrap loose thoughts I can't make sense of
So tired of it
Lazy with words now
Trying to fit stories in verse
Few things make it to the outline
Fewer to its ending
What do you want from me
What now?

Who Cares

One pill or two
I crashed my car and still don't see it
Who cares
Just another ordinary act of the life that pushed me away
A handful feels even better
I was somewhere in my head
When it happened.

Dropping back quickly
For a glass of wine or two
And a fight or two
Who cares
It's all the same with you.

What Happened

I forget where we first met
Was it Rome at Caesar's
I was a dancer and you're a drunk asleep on a table
Or in that Parisian afternoon
Through the revolving doors of a cafe
The Savannah trip maybe
As I was dying on the road from a snake bite
Or at the Romanovs
Lost on the steppes as I was looking for God
Perhaps in my dreams
A king and a queen
We're royals at the time
Surprisingly happy
Ordinarily loud.

What happened next
For how many years
A jungle of narratives follows me around
Like an open book that I try not to read
Others do it for me
With the mad passions of beasts
Hunger I never thought possible
I fear for my soul waking up deaf
As the crowd still stashes my voice away
Am I allowed at least the right to forget?

In time
Like time
We just exist
And have done it all
Have we really
I don't recognize truth any longer
Or its worth.

It's time to die
Wake up somewhere else
Fall in love with strangers
Live a life.

This one
I want so bad to forget.

First Coffee, Then Wine

First coffee
Then wine
I wasn't looking for illusions
Nor bending truth into comfort lies
The wind waltzes
The wine doesn't yield much
Where does all the vine listening go to
I wonder
Maybe you know.

I still hear you around
Why
I'm human after all
All out of patience with persisting absurdities
Thought dies beyond reality lines
The wind still waltzes
Still stubborn the wine
Where does all the vine listening go to
I wonder.

Strolling the Seine

I close my eyes
To stop this world from spinning
Behind the curtains I see you
Can't tell in light or darkness.

Would I still spot you
If night had not visited or was it gone
Wrapped in winter you're not a love blessing
I know this much.

Ride a rollercoaster now
Winds woven into tracks
Lean back tight
Would it ever stop
Would we land holding hands.

Beauty long gone
Only a dry cough left behind by the past cold
No wonders either
The sequence's already played out
I'm strolling the Seine alone.

Am I liberated
The world refuses to let loose its ropes
I flag no regrets
No peace either
Just reading the Seine
At surface we meet
You fisting foam
Me longing for the deep.

The thought now
Like a dull pain bothers me

If only I could drown it in the Seine.

(Paris, Dec2021)

You Again!

You're a departure
Why still wondering here
Who said I'm a gate
Ready on smile for the next check in
Don't walk my way
I don't like where u come from
Distance I can't cut with glass
Too much I can't cross
I'm Cote d'Or
Red whispering
You're just a daddy
Mind your sugar in the cup
That role requires some fitting
Had me in your heart you said
Came to see where I sat
Would you clean next time you ask guests over
I almost fell on dirty floors and string traps
Did you have to crash on me
I was barely standing even then
A wreck doesn't need more speed
Please take the nonsense away
What do I do now with the words in my head
Can't put them down, I hate flashlights
I can't laugh
I can't cry
In the abyss between
Help me fly them high.

If All of You Is All of Me

I gave your name to the sand
And it passed it on to the wind
I wrote it on the shore
And the wave had it in a few sips
The water didn't even let me finish it.

I called your past loves
Sure a few letters can fit in some corner of their sheets
No space they said
Too many washes the sheets had seen
They're too thin to carry history.

I threw it at you
And you let it drop in the air
A few versions already in pockets perhaps.

What do I do now
I want it somewhere where I can see
And I can't if there's no distance
If all of you is all of me.

This Nonsense of Me, This Nonsense of You

You were my thought
That walked in verses
On white sheets of paper
That the paper forgot
Words were not needed
For you and I.

I don't remember much
Is it fog or steam
We made love
Its anatomy now lost on me
Only the whisper I still hear in my blood.

Sheets on the floor
Like crumpled paper
Or is it all paper
Is it all thought
Ah this nonsense of me
In this nonsense of you
Again got lost...

Almost.

Because You Don't End…

Few minutes before my next flight
I can still smoke one
Why did I even start
Ah yes
Prince Charming
I hear one needs a few rolls when you're around
And I loved you
I fell for nothing
Still my favorite falling
Couldn't leave for all the disaster
I wonder why I met you
I believe in causes, not destinies
Perhaps that poem in the beginning
Was all the telling
All the reading
You're still the talk
Of this village and the one next to it
Last night they laughed you off in Italian
Do you still do chicken and beer on Friday nights
Sad you never made it further in life
I haven't done any better either
Still flying on Spirit
First class lifestyle if not seating
Don't remember much of what I told my head
In that airport seat
All in smoke
Burning the noise behind my back
Perhaps rage will stop by again another day
I'll tell you what it said
Because I want to finish you
And you don't end…

A Snowflake

You're a snowflake
He softly whispered
And my head jumped on one in silence.

I thought
I don't want to fall on your hair
Scared to get lost in your thoughts
Let me lay on your tongue
If you've never tasted snow
Or hold me on your hand
So I can melt on your skin
Oh, just let me sit on your lips.

I said
I only fall as one
Like in a ballet
In silence and shapes
Never pieces
I pretend it's simple when I'm tired
Trying to let complexities be the rug under my feet
Not the fire consuming all the living.

Beautiful like a crystal
Was all I meant he said
And I regretted
Not getting lost in his thoughts instead.

Leave the Crowd of Me

It bothers me to see you
Wear names snatched of my head
Tony's no longer around
Has been awhile since Sopranos gave him the last hug
And I took back New York
And Paris
Paris writes jokes on your name tag.

I walked to solve
Now can't help walking the walk
Still you around my steps
Feels like dating the gym instructor
One without the looks or the muscle
I collect such flirts for club laughs
The only membership in my keychain is a library card.

Leave the crowd of me
Has been dark for too long
Beauty is all I need.

When My Shadow Leaves

What's left in us
When our shadow falls on the ground
The past thin and flat laying down
The future still negotiating with the skies
And the thunder of the present connecting the dance.

Between a woman and her shadow
Stands her desire
I used to think
If you're my thunder
You're all I am
When my shadow falls on the ground.

I Don't Mind it

When you touch me
You send me somewhere I forget to tell
Words get lost
Sounds die in the air
A thousand birds escape away
I'm afraid if you're still with me
Or did I leave you behind

Do touch me anyway.

Days Like This

In days like this
I want to do nothing
And just think of you
Empty all the rooms
Throw out the agendas and the hours of light
Cancel time travel and wishes of the night.

In days like this
I can do nothing
Can't even find myself
To send around for errands or ask for favors
Maybe because I'm visiting your thoughts
Maybe there's a universe of us somewhere.

Don't

Don't break into my evening
If you left in the night
Slamming doors
Cursing loud
Down the stairs riding horses
Dragging me to the public square.

Is the applause the triumph of your soul
Did you enjoy enough noise
Or other expos are still in works
How much more in the script to follow
Maybe I can act the show.

I think some
Write less
Even less I speak
Without commentary
My head's the only reality that exists.

Don't push me into more thinking
Tell me I'm a fool
That stepped into your game
So I can feed peace to doubts
And walk another way.

I still talk to you sometimes
Have you forgotten my name
That's okay
It's the order of things
Not a thing to order
Orders - noise I don't have anyway.

Ride along cowboy

FIVE YEARS IN HELL

I heard enough
Even more I didn't
If in crossroads we ever happen to be
Don't bother for a nod
Strangers wouldn't be too far from reality.

Jamming with Strangers

Whiskey and chocolate throw me on the wheel
Red leather seats only compliment me
I drove all evening
Passed O'Hare
Yet fog's all I hit in the morning
Am I even somewhere.
...

What are you saying
You read me all wrong
Shall I blame it on the cheap alcohol
It was a soul rendezvous
Not a liver affair
On a cocktail napkin
Thought's not thin
Only the paper.

Shoot some Plato on my leather
To cut me off day dealings
Or join my ride
Or my rain
And hear my tears of ignorance or pain
Loved the jamming
What you're up to tonight
I prescribed myself rooftops
My doctor would not understand
High air sways free of knots.
...

Where do I get a preview of the human soul
History closed doors on me
Floods of confusion
Can you help

The drink's on me at the Hermitage
Marble tempting never fades on me like that of thick silk
O'Hare can use a few days for planning
I'm already there
Mediocrity here cuts like a knife
What moves my blood now
Damn this life!
…

It should be simple
Amen
It's heavy on my end
Is it still life when I search for it
The depth of thought now eluding me
Whiskey allows no competing attractions
Opening thoughts end up in fractions
Why bother either
I see no arguing
We meet by the same river
Rafting same conclusions to the shore
I don't get it
Why the past like the river runs ahead for more
Help me, I'm lost
Few late nights at the club
Fewer moments that carry away
All sober am I now
Still chasing life
All wrong, so wrong
Sleep's the only friend I want.
…

Half awake
Half asleep
Which side is this reading
Neither dreams nor days have dared this much
I need O'Hare

We rhyme so well together
Had forgotten excitement
You already got a monument in my head
On airplane schedules now
I don't even have a dress
Should one feel a high schooler again
What am I thinking
But when did much thought bring me the good life
I don't have a choice
But to follow a smile.

(Nashville 2023)

How I Like It

I can't write since I wake up with you
Expected otherwise
Thought you'd be life
This new thing I'd rush to tell about
My ticket finally in this world
For a heaven ride.

Not happening
I fall on you and there's no next
Does time stop when there's no memory of it
Or do I lose my mind or my breath
If I don't know or I can't tell.

Hold me
Hold me light
Your touch barely leaning on me
And let me burn
Wild
A bit longer
The sweet burn of ecstasy.

Back to the dinner table now
What show to watch next
Do you mind grabbing some wine
And where's your jacket
Need to look through pockets again
For my breath or my mind.

Part 4: In Stubborn Search of a Smile

Inside Out

Blue skies lay out of my window
Uncomplicated
Undisturbed
What are you up to I wonder
What's in the wink.

The wind laughs my window away
The sheets tie a hammock in the sky
On a cloud I rest
Following light that crumbles on the ocean
To a lazy boat waiting for the sunset.

Silence like after-love
Give me a moment to breathe it in
Is this all real
Truth rejects easy answers
I don't care if it's all a dream.

I want to wear the moment inside out
Lay the dream on my skin
The sheets in tear to dry in the sky
If only the space was my roulette
And I could send off despair to another time.

Another Drink

A bit drunk am I
So what
No wait
Thank you heavens
I need wings to reach the next moment
And the next after that
As close as I can to forever.

I'm an immigrant
Like anyone else
Time I travel to
Time I leave behind
If bridges between hours are too weak to walk
Better if I fly.

Maybe a song as I walk through
Takes me dreaming
Takes me places
Takes me faces.

I stretch on clouds
How do I get my feet up there
The thought makes me laugh under my hat
My daughter can't stand its sound
Still respecting this world
She can't have me sticking my tongue out at it
The innocence!
When did I lose it.

Did I
I think of myself as its loyal fan
Still trysting dreams
Still full of dreams

Where was I in the dream
…
Ah, maybe another drink.

(Miami 2021)

About a Wave and a Shore

Sipping espresso by the ocean
While the morning was still asleep
Silence wrapped around my shoulders
And silver skies sat next to me.

Happy laughs all gone
Alone facing the immensity
Like a pile of clothes I left my body at the shore
And flew towards the wonder.

Couldn't see my tears coming
Lonely, then in storms
Maybe the wave got in me
Pushing reality out of my soul.

Words left me-
Small vessels of meaning are they after all
On knees I prayed
Speechless
The moment was the word.

The wave left me for the shore
Same desires of her at every travel
Falling on him she lost herself
He wondered how to hold the moment forever.

I thought of love
Of love rocks usually people rave
Of a shore I dreamed-
A million sanded rocks walking through time to their waves.

(Miami 2021)

Shut Up

Think I saw a rat today
A rat with a pink phone
That sat next to me
Loud
Talking dreams
Imagining lions
Something I've known in another life
Poor rat
Stop whining
All animals are not equal
You still don't know that
Paint your nails
Hit the open road
Be of some service somewhere.

Black in Pink

A small notebook
Travels the corners of my life
Bags
Pillows
Pockets
All of an elf
A shrink
And a friend
All of my own.

Yes
My middle years
Dripping schedules
And shopping lists
Date nights
Anniversary themes
School bakes
And cooking recipes.

No
That's another time
Someone else's life
Mine is a miss
Dear notebook
I'm sorry you fell in my abyss.

I start writing somewhere in the middle
Can't stand screams since page one
Or let ghosts off too soon
It doesn't feel right.

My notebook gets me
Covers my eyes in pink

Softly holds my hand
Such tempting body extremes
I don't know what's louder
Its crying or my laughter.

Grace's Secret

(2 oz London Dry Gin, 1 oz Red Italian Vermouth, 1/3 oz Elderflower Liqueur, 2 dashes of peach bitters, lemon twist for garnish - courtesy of Peaky Blinders)

It broke
The glass pieces all over the floor
The mountain cried for his flowers
I cried for my daughter for long.

Trembling over the Tuscan hills
The vines sobered in shock
Artemisia in anger dropped the sword
I cried for my daughter for long.

In dismay the Brits sipped from their glasses
'These thieves!'
Gin first, now Shakespeare
In horror the Greeks grabbed the lemons
And ran to hide their tragedies.

The old magic envied this bitter
Were peaches that made the difference
Which side- the green or the orange
Even Benjamin doesn't seem to know.

The daughter left with the broken pieces
Ah well, farewell
Life they call it
Birth and death in it
And an ocean of pain in between.

A Visit at the MET

WIG also means Wildly Important Goals

Wigs behind crystal windows
Sitting high
Big and small
In tantalizing laces
Colors and shapes off a kaleidoscope.

Royals of self made kingdoms
Spice market variety of them
Is that all
Disastrous cooks
What's satisfaction in spice-only dishes served.

Phaethon's chariots flying high
This time burning the sun down
What were the Gods thinking
This goal's wild
The run for it too
Please
Please let the WIGs be
The last letters in this alphabet of madness.

Stories of the Living

Blues were defeated
Exalted reds marched the sky
The Gods were amused with the show
While an unpretentious moon claimed the night her own.

Naked
Full
In scarlet breaths
She sat on the water lips.

Tell me night
What did you see
Why take her away you shameless thief
What burning envies you couldn't let be.

Black magic melted her into a coin
Tossed amongst the stars
What is the reading
Yet light she still was
All the light
This traveler ever needed.

Degrees of Separation

Spectacles of sand in a stretch of beach
That is us
Insignificant degrees of physical separation
The distances between can only be reasoned
The other's pulse is all there is to feel.

Yet in the joint
Blind we lay to the distances
And the degrees of separation
Of the worlds stacked within.

So close
And so far
Why we never learn.

A Rainy Thursday in July Smelling like Cinnamon

If I could refine this Thursday
Change it in a Friday dress
Then waltz it back to Wednesday
More floor
More dancing would be left.

If I could refine this July
That still cries the stories of May
Hide its September perfume of spices and sweet
And their inevitable melancholy
Then I could
Perhaps restore its passion heat.

Structure of Me

I'm a tree and its birds
Rooted on this bench
In this lazy suburb
Along this silver pond
Where off to next.

In pieces I fly
Don't know destinations
Or how long
On that rock
On that star
On that thought.

In a million pieces
I rotate in the air
Falling down
On that church
On this messy hair

All here
All there.

Letter to Ferdinand Pessoa

You sound familiar
How do I know you
Have we met somewhere
Perhaps the breeze carried your soul
On the sweat of my parents' bed.

Sometimes we walk the same circles
On a picnic blanket I daydream too
Playing solitaire with confusions and roles
Ran over daily like a highway
Still carrying the indifference of a resigned soul.

Oh come on
Let's keep it fresh
It was Lisbon
The bookstore and the handshake
The sidewalk cafe
A drink then two
My daughter napping on the couch waiting.

Not easy for me to get rid of sentimentalism
Sometimes I go through our pictures
Chat with them
And I can't help but wonder
If the picture is just the physics of our encounter.

A Christmas Wish

Indifferent I walk by the feast outside
A sparkle is all I wish to hold
Slipping through my fingers
Softly falling into my soul.

Spirit talk to me
Can't trust my mind
Beaten for too long
Deep might be the scars of thought.

Shoot me a sparkle
And light me up
Let it be the summer of my soul
It is all this Christmas I ask for.

Listen Grace

I dream riding down an open road
And be all the good things
Weightless like the air
High like the sky
Game like the wind.

Chained to the wall
There are no shadows what I see
I lived the Republic
I touch reality.

Can't stand the knowledge
The geometry of pain I despise
The views ahead
Time and space anew
Hide the chance of a smile.

Down an open road
I dream being the ride
When thought like river never runs back
Or bothers to stop either.

It's been awhile my dear
Since I hit the open road
A forever since I breathed free
Would it be too much to ask
To toast in the sky
To the hope of the new
And the happiness of being with you.

On the Sideway

A sideway paved with rocks
Is my daily routine
The throw on my daily life too
It doesn't yield
Jammed with edges and forbidden borders
It plays on my soul
Like a dirty chess field.

Why life if it doesn't give living I wonder aside the
border cracks
Full of autumn leaves and
Shells of unfinished thought
How do we get used to misery
As time passes by us
Standing on the sidewalk.

2022
I refuse your fields
My soul's not meant for your misery
Holding on a dream
I watch my thought falling in the cracks
Slipping into a light passage
Serendipitously
Perhaps.

I start Friday with a Sunset

Started Friday with a sunset
The usual me
Distances don't matter
From a life on the negative
I can still dream.

Playing solitaire with my guesses
What is happiness
You have to be an ace
To be in my game
What is happiness
Escaping the prison in my head
Becoming the air on my face
I don't know
Has been a while to still tell
I'm lazy for other lineup of events
Afterall
I started Friday with a sunset.

Guesses

I never quite understood mornings
Do I leave the dream on my pillow
And this beach walk is meant to be life
Or do I wake up into a dream
And life is left behind asleep.

Waves wipe off the shore inside my head
I can use the extra space
Learn a new language perhaps
Happiness dances in my new space
If this a dream
Never do I want to be awake.

Chasing light
The heart forgets me
One less worry I think relieved
If this is life
Never again do I want to dream.

I can't know
Do I even need to
It's a philosopher's task where life and dreams collide
The morning felt perfect for a cigarette
And I smoked a thought instead.

Whose Company to Keep

Slow walking
Stumbling behind
My head refused the day
Like a lazy child I had to drag it around.

I didn't know whose company to keep
The hours or the mind
No reason to rush
Not much to crave on the memory side.

Perhaps the headache pill
Thought to sleep problems away
And negotiated distancing the head from the day.

Back and forth
Not exactly waltzing when the heart's not singing
Not exactly trouble when the head's away from the thinking.

Sunday Guesses

The seagulls didn't run away as I walked by
I wonder when's the last time I read obituaries
Am I ether souling around
Or are they memories standing by.

A thought of no practical consequences I guess
This crowd is all the life that I see
Just added a mental note in my calendar
To start reading newspapers and obituaries.

Silly Wishes

Don't let me fall on the day
Shouldn't a silly wish be easier to grant
I don't understand much of the ask either
Confusion, even silent, scares away butterflies of meaning.

It can be some nonsense
Or miracle
Like -
Let the time I live in be the time I deny
Though I wonder then
Where would life reside
Where would thought lay down
If there's no space of time.

It's late in the evening now
Not much left in the day to fall on
And I'm too busy with a recipe book
I knew a silly wish would be easy after all.

Hiking

I love this place
An ivory tower outside one
If only I could carry it with me
There's not enough space of thought for its beauty
It's an affair for the senses that refuses outlets
Except perhaps the memories rack
The word can't tell much either
The beauty's from beyond
While the letter from this world.

Glowing light
Walking down mountains
Flowing on rivers
Whispering on leaves
Singing with birds
And waltzing with the winds
Is this the love hug
Keeping the earth around for so long.

I want to do nothing
I suppose it means absenting the world on the move
And moored on the skyline
Have enough of a few important truths.

At Some Point

At some point
The rain got bored
And became afternoon
The nap worn itself out
Traveling places it didn't know
Talking to faces it didn't remember
It brought back
The win of an arm wrestle with a man on a kitchen table
Then the evening became tears
Did I pick it up where God left it
Washing away the writing in the dark
Time like paper like light
Was dressed in white.

Premium Fake

The city flashes premium fake
Premium craft's enough of a feeling they say
Oh dismiss the chorus
Just another deception
Got no patience for doubles appeal
In lost and found
I return all else
And keep the real.

Few truths
Too many screens
What to make of this living
I asked God at every church
Yet saints never left their walls
Would rather waste myself in daydreaming.

The city flashes premium fake
Premium craft's enough of a feeling they say
Make some room on the shelf
Would you
Here's a diagnosis
And spread the crowds on the fake bags too.

(Tirana 2023)

Wish I Could Invent a Language

Wish I could invent a language
Where words would be open skies
Not village boats
Holding so little
Wrecking so quickly
Failing intensity
Always slow for the sailor's soul
Never fit for immensity.

Wish I could invent a language
Where drawings would be space
Not shrugged maps
Of beaten down living
Of lines too weak to extend much
Ever missing the unknown
Ever missing the yearning marks.

This tower doesn't do it for me
The bones ache within.

A Heart with Boots

It happened
Notices were not sent
Or I missed them blinded by the storm
My heart wore boots
Jumping loud and wide
In deafening beats
Less of a dance
More of a madness thrill.

There's no rain inside
Or let's pretend
Walk out of them
And hold my hand
In light and dark
Love is the only fashion for the heart.

The effort fell like dust
My freedom became theirs
Now I don't know what to fear more
Their loud pounding
Or the thought of them
Walking outside my walls.

Just Don't Tell Me It's the Time of My Life

Give me one hour
One hour is all I ask
Of fantasy reality
And forgotten pasts
One hour
To feel the sunrise in my soul
And ascend on the horizon.

Still on the shallows
So far from the shore
On an error equation
The breath dies short.

Wanted to catch fireworks from the Eiffel Tower
Champagne toasts and wet kisses
Burn all the other maps
Won't meet at kilometer zero in Paris
Need no heels to stand tall
But under the bridge I'd still pick up a Vogue
And my Manolos deserve a better mile
A better walk.

Is this the finish line someone asked
What's the run
Forget interlocutors of no trust
Won't meet behind sick walls
I tell you this much
Still haven't put the Christmas presents away
And wasn't summer savage enough.

What year is this
Is this still time
Only the rivers seem still flowing

Lie to me
Just don't tell me
It's the time of my life.

Smiles

I sought the company of smiles
Those made of light
Oblivious to all
Smiles that take you on the dancing floor
That make the thought forget
And the troubles themselves ignore.

I wish I was you
So I could smile for me
Or be my sleep
Order the right dreams in
Could have been transactional
Though shops sell lamps not light
But why Epcot with Paris still around.

I painted then
I painted smiles
Out of every light in the dark
Neons and stars
Could't tell them apart.
A symphony of smiles
That I dare not finish
And I carry it around with me
Always writing
Always reading.

Part 5: Hope or Something Like It

Mercy

I wish the world was like this church table
Balanced on a cross
Despair laying down with no after
And the good returning
Toasting with wine and laughter.

I wish pain was like this candle
Burning itself down
Lighting up the way
And the spirit of a new day.

I wish my heart was like this church
Full of saints and victories earned
A cross for every battle fought
Telling the story of resurrection every year.

I wish my body was like this priest
Dressed in gold
In calm expecting death
Refusing space to worries
Filling the air with songs that never end.

Wishes
Soul sights
Like smoke flying
Heavy is the day
And mortal I'm still
Lord have mercy I pray.

Searching for a Poem Fallen from the Sun

I've been searching for a poem
Fallen from the sun
Nothing else I can take now
Circles in ashes
Like in water grow wide
Night, day, night
Why end where I started
Gains lost twice.
My pockets full of verses never finished
Children of sadness
I dread the endings they'll run
The faces they'll greet
I need to find a poem fallen from the sun.

How do I trace the orbit
With my head still walking yesterday's sorrows
Someone said 'put yourself on the back'
Maybe I'll do that
Then face a sunrise
And wait
Sitting on its path.

Water-Shaped

Bad memories
Their time does not break
It does not eat
Or drink
Or takes the kids to the park
Their time's destitute of life
Shade can only shape darkness.

Their time doesn't grow up either
Same orphan lunatic living on the street
Chasing people around
Wrapping their heads in his stink.

In their time
There's no more of the form I was
And on the ground
Nothing less than the shape of water
Will I stand another crack I fear
Assurances on a smile grow
Earthquakes bring down structures
Water will always flow.

Project X

I had this city in me
Like a rooftop pool
Bright
Warm
Like thoughts of spring
Or the pill in the wallet
For headache swings.

I don't remember how it happened
Delivered it like a stone
For my own hit
In my sleep walks
Pain?
Here's a bin if tears remain.

Long battles are said to burn a torch of madness
That changes sides
Passes hands
Where is it now
Who is to tell
I can't see
Too much ashes on heads.

I don't care if I don't see
Will take the city back either way I vow
Street by street.

(New York City, 2021)

Lunar Illumination

Will you roll out a beam of light on dark waters for me
I can send up a story
I don't want to climb all the way up
Not asking you to impress me
Not trying to impress you either
Don't bother for a chat
Not looking for a muse
Forget excitement
Just don't want you to fall asleep
So that I can drink your light a bit longer
Like a camel wandering the night dessert alone.

Guards to Executioners

Sometimes the world
Gets bored of elliptical walks around the sun
Tired
Drops commuters
From one station to the other
Forgets carrying them back
All sorts of stations
Sinners to saints
Angels to demons
Guards to executioners
A stranger crying on an unknown stone
Perhaps seeking her own solace from the road
Why I bother
Externalities of no importance to a soul looking after its own
Where can I jump on the swing is all I ask
Can I fly high a little
Just a little
Aristotle words suggest convincing
'Virtue is equal distance from opposites'.

Solve It!

I can't arrive at a new day
Carrying the walk with me at the door
Or carrying the bridges
That the past could cross
Not easy
The present's just a giant wheel
Rolling the past prison in
I hide in things and thinking
Is it still life
If it gives no living
I try to run fast
Yesterday even faster after me
How can I solve time
If mornings do no sorting
How can I solve time
If breathing wakes up
The present and the past alike.

A Birthday Card to Me

You're so lucky to have me
Have you ever thought of it
Our heart perhaps has
Have you ever thrown me hugs in the air
Or have faith for casual wear.

Not a sound off a raindrop
I'm creation descended on bird wings
Do you see that beach
That is me
The shore is my head
With uninvited visitors and too much noise
While like water I flow to distant islands
Where my legs meet to gossip.

That mountain
I'm that too
The forest is my head
My leaves throw shapes in the wind
As I flow down the valley
Where the gossip still reels.

Have you ever seen all this
Yes I know of pain, darkness, and fog
All the savage talk
They're just commas in a piece I write
So what
I always rewrite.

Human too
A page full of words
Words full of passion
I can write you a poem

If you love me just a little
If you can be my sky when storms knock in
Don't break the sentence
'Cause we're a beautiful page
Beginning to end.

I Believe

I want to wake up
Somewhere in my mind
Where I haven't been
Or trouble hasn't reached.

Be the stranger in me for awhile
And that's okay
I can trade securities
For the promises of desire.

Learn a new language
Just forget this one
If I can't silence the thought
At least I won't understand its talk.

An indifferent ignorant
How can I refuse the fortune of Eden
Let me toast with the gods
Pain no longer lives here.

Wandering as a tourist
Trivial is this atlas shape
Gossip for the world to see
Gossip I don't live in.

With thoughts under seizure
Yet boundless by inception
I take my luck
And still search for peace
Yes, I believe.

On the Road Again

On the road again
I've lost count how many times now
Chasing freedom I told myself
And I was
In dreams and cry.

Back in the old town
Perhaps this church can bless on me
Its signature peace of sleeping conflicts
All too weak to hold my hand on the street
I laugh around
Don't understand why I'm here
The hell's kitchen comes with no treats.

I reach for my father's smile behind his stone
Let me live on that ray a bit longer
Here's a cigarette to share
A candle too
A prayer burning for me
A prayer burning for you.

From afar
Across the fields
The lake breaks into my chest
Letting loose mind and soul
My bad luck-
Their road's never far from the storm
Behind its curtain
Like this mountain are disappearing tomorrows.

Nothing noteworthy I like to think
Sipping my usual espresso
Doing the usual things

Weather and wars chatting
Searching for the mountain behind the storm
Like a mirror of myself still standing.

(Korca, Pogradec Sept. 2022.)

Writing & Erasing

Paper looks better in white I convinced myself
Like the other side of trouble
Or a weekend getaway
Undisturbed by thought traps and puzzles.

Hang words around
On people watching and story guessing
Or send thoughts away
To fantasy lands on beauty searches.

Temptations of rain whispered the hour
Is there a shelter in its crossroads
A place other than my despair for it to fall
There's not much comfort in the touch of wet clothes.

Only paper on my hands
All in ropes like an exorcism ritual
Is it the rain or my thought slashing harder
I wonder.

Perhaps I can fool this hour
Though only lies can fool
Can win its melancholy argument perhaps
Why write in rain
If it only melts paper away
If it only writes what it ends up erasing.

In the Gangsters' Paradise

Let me go
You should go
I don't have to pray for freedom
Don't know how to trade for it
It's madness to ask
Yet on my knees
I beg for a pact.

The shade of delusions and illusions thick on my head
I reach for air
Telling myself shade is not weight
Just darkness flat on pavement.

In the gangsters' paradise
Only the fool is now dead
But I gave you the fool to save myself
And redemption
Not your money I want
I don't know how to tradeoff
Why the tradeoff.

I can't breathe
A fist of air-
Between my fire, the winds, and my lungs
Is never enough
You should go
Life, freedom, redemption
Now.

Inspire Me Please

Inspire me
Tell me something beautiful
New
Something I haven't seen or heard
Take all of me away and leave trouble behind
Carry my soul into light.

There is no time
Agonies linger on the ground
You say it's not about me
Who made me about you
A sad object to play
Why do you even have a saying.

I thought spirit meant good things
And law not a paperback
Yeah, I finished the book
Not its living
The exhibitionist carousel in dizziness
Still spinning.

Inspire me
Lift the shadows of past tags on my wrists
Leave this carnival behind
Throw me into desire wings
And if not off to a new life
Pull me on a thought at least.

Tell me something beautiful
Inspire me
Please.

No Right Card

Read too much on these stands
And still don't have your birthday card
It's all too small
My heart won't fit in
Not because I'm a perfectionist
Just because I love you too much.

Wish I could give you the world
The best that is
The beauty of the sunrise
And the rhythm of spring
The determination of storms
And the passion of sunsets
And have the diamond in your heart
Baptize in strength your thought and blood
But why the wish
The words are written on you
It's so easy to see.

I wish you knew no tears
Or thought it was the rain outside
Wish you never had to reach for a pill
Or fall on a bad memory
But why the wish
Today
I can veil indifference to the pain.

Happiness then
I wish you happiness
Bright as light
Immense like your heart takes over the sky.

Still I have no card

Wouldn't change much had I carried the whole stand
Something would still be missing
I'd still be searching around
Not because I'm a perfectionist
Just because I love you too much.

I can't find the right card
Wish I could envelope the love in my heart.

You Always Can

I never understood your birthday blues
I'm tired now to search libraries
And is too late for the wish.

Scared of growing up you say
Can I come closer and pass on a secret
This world frightens me too
What if tomorrow
Falls on the present like morning dew
I don't fear the unknown
Just the thought of the present taking over tomorrow.

I don't know much
I'm just a stash of questions on some shelf of time
And time is funny
With its cyclical runs
And January resets
Wiping off the past.

Child of change
If tomorrow turns to lemonade
Chilling a tiring present
Throw it off your party
And start rewriting.

Promise me
Next time this world wears you out
You'll remember to change it
You always can
And heavens will be by your side
Because you were born
As God was rewriting time.

Inevitably

Driving around
The night is cold and wet
I know these streets
Their tall buildings and low act.

Inevitably
What are we if not memories
I fall in the past
Fall on the street
Wish we're not driving around here
On my daughter's birthday
Wish I had peace
Tonight you're running all over me.

I searched for life around here
Pushed and fooled
Abused by many
A soul bleeding itself
Holding on to the memory of me
Frightened to think will it again be me.

Tracing steps now
Pain doesn't allow words
Except a thought
Your dangerous feast on my sanity
Its savage laugh
Did it end its walk
The contours of the buildings
Now lost in the dark
Perhaps God's sealing their fate of being one.

Inevitably
What are we if not standing

I rise on the moment
Up from the street
Let's go for a ride, shall we
A Scorpio bar around here is still open for a drink
Before once again
We run over these streets.

I'm an Amateur

Skipping the present
Still dark outside after all
What hour of the night are you
And how did I end up in these streets
You'll fade away
It's all that I read in the night's DNA.

Not much I can offer
Respect is for another life
Sit if you wish
Like an hourglass I can put hate aside
Let me hear your story
What is that you want
Five minutes is all you got
And it's dripping along.

Don't call my name
I'm not coming
Reflecting on its death
The bull would never run after red
I followed you around
Around is not a destination
Just whirlwind dizzying light existence
I'm only light as in shining
Done a lot of journey too
Now longing for the view.

Here's a pearl melting in wine
And a toast to my health
Just as they did in ancient times
I'm not a Cleopatra nor a queen
Just a random woman in her right to live.

FIVE YEARS IN HELL

Time slipped away
I'm back at my desk
Still no story
Doubt there was beaty to regret
Am I not playing it right
Call me an amateur if you like
Here's a dictionary
It only means
I'm passionate about my life.

A Woman I Know

I know that little girl in the park
Schoolbag silent by her side
She reads stories
Leaves the bench for the pages sometimes
Late for dinner on the way home.

I know that girl
The book forgotten behind
Seeing stories in sheets of winds hanging around
Filing them in the sky
Riding clouds.

I know that woman
A pass thrown in her bag
Reading time scripts wrapped in dreams
Sadness sits heavy in the glass of the afternoon turn
And somewhere deep in her heart
Where cognac can't reach to burn.

Impossible on the shelf the binder
I ripped it off in thousand pieces
Each piece in a thousand more
From my window saw them drifting into oblivion
The past that no longer even the past was
And if it deceives
I'll do it a hundred thousand times more.

I close my eyes
Roll on nets of lights dancing wild
Skipping a present still held somewhere I can't reach
Can't reason any better
And wink to the sky for a book of magic.

Let me hold thunder
To shatter down this prison, its shadows
Burn the miles to the daughter standing next to me
And let flames reveal a new world
Born in wish.

P.S. Skipping the present
       Will you read the book of magic to me?

Why Do You Make Me Leave This Chair

Why do you make me leave this chair
It still annoys me
Silence please as I walk through the hall
Be bad and loud
Behind closed doors.

Chances don't take away choices
The handshake of an encounter laying winter on my hand
Won't make it upstairs
In my head
I promised myself that
Drunk on oyster air
A certain mood like a blanket wraps me today
The other stories can wait
For awhile I'll join this sway.

I'm the opposite sex
Not sex opposed
But tonight I'll let my bedroom go to sleep on a different smoke
How are you I ask myself
A habitual 'fine' does not convince
'Indifferent to noise' sounds better
Hopeful in a quest for peace.

I should feel some degree of triumph
I do not
Why the battles we don't start ourselves
Make peace feel akin to obsolete
Or am I naive
Wouldn't be worse to burn in a fire you didn't start
What would that losing be.
(Women's Int'l Day 2023)

Four Hours in Rome

Take me to the Colosseum first
On a thrill ticket and audience seats
Or allow me a hit
Let years of pain weigh on my fist.

It makes no sense
Nothing around me does
The plane wine still gives my tongue a flex
On a flight to Rome
Will I wait for Rome I ask.

Sometimes I feel as running out of time
Can you run out of what you don't have
An empty coke between my angry knees
Writes a loud X
Like a variable of uncertainties.

There's advice in the pages of history
Come as a catholic to win this city
I pray on a cross to send away doubts
Only four hours in Rome
And the thought is a smile.

The sun will rise to land me
Just a schedule thing that my foolish heart will blend into meanings
I come from conflict
Ease me into beauty
Can't run far from faith in streets
Where church bells wake up the city.

Tigers and Ferraris-
Caged speeds within the city walls

I walk around meanings I cannot reach
My father's saint used to patron around here
Rome, free me
Redeem me.

(Rome 2023)

I'll Fly

I can
I will
There's always immensity beyond
Forget the limits you think you reached
Soar till beauty's in sight
The Soul is meant to fly
Does it become a fantasy
Or a fantasy it follows
When it all wears out
And lost is hope.

I'll fly
Airplanes shine brighter than stars in the night sky
Dressed in the sparkles
Of life excitement
And new horizons.

Born of meaning this life
I see it all taken down now
A clown's laugh rings at my ear instead
My own clown the loudest
While I search for the end.

I lend my arm to the air
And hold the mountain on my hand
Rest my head on a bible
And hear doors opening in the sky
The worlds of yesterday I no longer see
Collapsed in waves
Cities conceived in sin.

(Korce 2023.)

Effervescent

I.

Dead ends and wrong turns
Time lost
Do words even make sense
The lost things still wander in the world up for grabs.

Can't leave the bed
Soft pillows or harsh realities
Blameless
Guilt - free
I'm not trading
Who ever can
Daily love can still visit in my head
Even better
Devoid of physics
Perfection spreads wings
Fairytales are real
And I fall asleep on a champagne bubble
Flying over the drowning.

II.

Another missed sunrise
How can my soul walk on rooftops now
And leave this world behind
Life still calls when you're alive
Someone said
But I lose the thread to silly cartoons laughing off a text
Is that what it meant.

Wake me up when there's another Creed
Someone's throwing the punches I can't

A justice language still
I can conversate with that
Better yet
Punch the stage down
Need the roar of an upheaval
Forget your drilling inside my head
I'm the Monaco sky
Worlds away from this village belt of broken shells.

I deserve beauty for once
A justice language still
My God.

The October Diary

Playing Russian roulette with my pen
Perhaps fate will give me a shot
The cross on my hand traveled new lines
As time rolled by.

Wishing upon a candle now in a dim hotel room
Flames burning on silky sheets
Far 's the whisper of rain behind my window
And love dreams taint the melancholy.

Save me tonight
What am I if not faith
Not looking for smart conversations
Just a true connection
Desire and ease are all I want to be.

Why am I here
The October sun doesn't give away my reasons
Everyone else walks behind a mask
Was I born when life was meant to be hidden.

Take me back to the rhythm of my beginning
Some beauty to breathe I beg
I can dance with a vampire
If my heart goes out on fire.

War echos from afar
Fill the emptiness around me
Shall I write or drink a toast on my day
Need a beautiful illusion if not reality.

Light me up
And carry me away

Fly me high on love
Stop the clocks for a breath or a sight
Though their difference escapes me now.

The room drowns in loud beats
And me in adrenaline like on a life vest
Scattered at shores of nowhere at the end
Under naked skies behind the smoke of the rain.

No postcards to Self in print
Am I not allowed to knock on my own door
Those on the floor say nothing
The velvet of red roses on my face 's the only comfort.

I'll better write one
Listening to midnight sips
And wishing for a different time zone
There's no happiness in those in me.

The days went
After the falling leaves
Or the birds that left
Ever more void around
I never understood my fatal attraction with them
Like a lover I can't stop talking
Or a gone soul that can't help memories calling.

All in my head
Still burning
Like the fire I lit last November
Still praying
Light me up
And carry me away.

Pse Erdha

(The October has to speak in Albanian too)

Harruar jam ne rulete ruse me penen time
Mbase fati ende ruan per mua nje plumb
Kryqi ne pellembe zgjati vija te reja
Ndersa vitet me rradhe humben.

Lutem ne nje dhome te muget hoteli
Flaket e qiririt harbojne ne carcafe te mendafshte
Fjalet e shiut pas qelqi nuk me arrijne me
Kaq shume melankoli
Kaq pak dashuri.

Shpetome sot
Une ende besoj
Nuk me duhen dialoge interesante a te rreme
Fjale shpirti kerkoj
Deshire dua te jem.

Pyes pse jam ne kete bote
Dielli i tetorit arsyet ne arkiva hequr
Ku te gjej pak bukuri
Te shkruaj a pi nje urim ne diten time
Iluzion a realitet nuk ka rendesi.

Nuk gjeta dot kartoline per vete
Nuk me lejohet te trokas ne deren time?
Letrat mbi krevat thone gjera te merzitshme
Kadifeja e trendafilave te kuq- e vetmja prehje e imja.

Degjoj veren pas mesnate
Dhe vetes i shkruaj
Lutem kaq shume per nje tjeter kohe
Hapesire pa lumturi ato qe kaluan.

Beme drite
Dhe percillme
Percillme ne lumturi
Ndaloji oret per nje fryme a psheretime
Ndonese diferencen nuk e kuptoj tani
Beme drite lutem
Beme drite
Dhe larg percillme.

Pretend Simple

I know storms live in silent clouds
And dazzling ice crystals kiss in frost bites
Just the way it is
There's no deceit
Except perhaps in our thoughts
Pretend it's simple I tell myself
What if simple is meant to accept complexities
As if at ease
And step ahead
Throwing our shape in the kaleidoscope
Leaving auditioning thoughts at the gate
And witness the possible
Its infinity
Silent when lights are down
Breaking the glass
When no longer can help screaming.

ABOUT THE AUTHOR

Ariola Molla is an Albanian- American in Boston, a woman, a mother, a lawyer, a cook, a traveler that doesn't travel enough, and mostly a dreamer that on a tough hand of cards couldn't help reflecting on emotional exhaustion, the intimate relationship with personal rights, the morality of power, and above all, the human potential and its randomness in surpassing limits in a relentless pursue of life.